Hard Gal Fi Dead
Musings, Poems, Notes to Self

Tami Tsansai

(Tameka A. Coley)

Hard Gal Fi Dead
Copyright © 2018 by Tameka A. Coley

ISBN-13: 978-1722844462
ISBN-10: 1722844469

Cover photo inspired by the Japanese Kintsukuroi perspective

Concept and Creative Direction: Tameka A Coley for Tsansai
Make-up (@tamitsansai)

Photography: Warren Alexander Buckle (@wabadude)

Cover design: Neil A. Buckle (@neilusandme)

Copy Editing: Janice Casserly (Write On!)

Formatting: Elijah Jean Editing (www.ElijahJeanEditing.com)

LIVICATION

Livicated to my mother Christine, my sister Keanu, my brother Howard, Mama, Ms. Coley, all the other women whose struggles I carry in my DNA; and my grandfather, Randall, who taught me at a very young age that being a woman is so much more than just 'pretty looks'. May his soul rest in peace, power and love.

HARD GAL FI DEAD

SUBSTANCE

Part I
MUSINGS (Volumes 1-3): thoughts, recollections
and emotions

Part II
POEMS: Sensory perception and elucidation

Part III
(LOVE)-NOTES TO SELF: and encouragement for
all (womb)men

ACKNOWLEDGMENTS

Dear phenomenal people in my life - whose love has shaped me - once again, my lovely grandmother, Una M. Brown (Mama), my loving aunties by blood and bond - especially Jackie, Tricia, Stephanie, Janice and Sharol, whose strength amazes me every day; Simone and Ashley, my 'ride or dies'; Miriam, my soul sister, without whom this book wouldn't have been published; Joanna, who always encourages me to be my truest self; the super-talented Stephanie Hava who gave me sound advice to get this book published, and has become one of my treasured friends; Rochelle who saved my life, always supports me and encourages my creative expressions.

Dr. Michael Bucknor, who extended the olive branch when it was most desperately needed; NMW, 'Miss Wint', Racquel, Nickalia, Ali, Michelle, Alley, Ayanna, George, Angie, Kadene, Sherece, Nicole, GiGi, Kareece, Mili, Chereese and Jhanille, all of whom have anchored me on different parts of my journey. The International Goddess Council - my 'sistas' - and of course, my sleeping beauty Kelli, a model of loveliness, strength and resilience. To Mallory and Ryo, who are always there to 'check' me when I need it; Solange Knowles, whose 'A Seat At The Table' album I took as a sign that this book is not 'too deep' to release from my clutches.

My 'one draws' guru in slumber, Robby P, the epitome of a friend and guide; my dear 'Uncle George' for his unwavering support; the amazingly talented artist brothers Wabadude & Neilus, my long-time 'family-friends' who did my cover, and my biggest teacher-in-love to date, now friend, Adam, from whom I learned - in splits, triumphs, simplicities and tumult!

Lastly and most importantly, to my wonderful sisters Keanu, Akilah and Britney, my amazing brother Howard, my charming and beautiful Mum, Christine Joy Brown, and all the other women worldwide who are kicking major ass against the odds. I salute you all - you inspire me. This book is for us.

HARD GAL FI DEAD

You pick him up, you lick him dung, him bounce right back. What
a hard man fi dead!
— Prince Buster, Hard Man Fi Dead (1966)

AUTHOR'S NOTE

Welcome to the front room of my mind; an autobiography - 31 years in the making. There's poetry inside full of beauty and pain, real excerpts from my journals, fuzzy and crystal-clear memories of true-to-life experiences, inspirations from the mental ward and beyond... all lessons I've gathered (and continue to explore), by living through them. It is informed by trysts with emotional traumas I thought I wouldn't ever survive; mired in my spiritual awakening and flavoured by the renewal I found immersing myself in the wonders of nature, music and cathartic writing.

In many ways my writing is dark, as honesty often is. I pour my thoughts, my emergence and awakening into these pages in the hope that you will come away from it feeling a little unsettled and a lot moved, enough, anyway, to have a conversation, if even with only yourself; or, at the very least to look inside, be totally unapologetic about, forgiving of, and kind enough to saturate in love that which is your true SELF. I am sharing my hard-hitting truths because I, like most women, have been through many trials; some constant, some occasional and have emerged bruised, but definitely better.

'Hard Gal Fi Dead' is designed to illuminate and celebrate how special it is to accept yourself and especially, to be a woman. We are strong, magical, powerful, amazing, magnificent, divine beings; gifted with the power to usher creation from one realm into the next; we are here to restore order and balance in a crazy time-space. When we acknowledge this, open our minds, stand in our truths and lift our voices, we will create a community of empowered, supportive, loving, awesome, badass women who can change the world. Thank you for reading.

Love, light and blessings. . .

—Tami

Musings...

Volume I

Purpose

The thing about passion is once you find it, you cannot
'un-feel' it
No matter how difficult the journey.

The wonder years: an ode to self-love

Oh darling!
How lovely it will be when you realise
Just how beautyfull you are.

Arguments

After the explosion
I realised loving someone means
having them jerk you awake.
Clean a giant mirror
And hold it up to your imperfect face.

Venus Fly Trap

One of the sweetest things about you,
lover
is when, barely awake
You address me incoherently
Fling your leg over me
Then ever so gently
Pull me in.

Volume II

HARD GAL FI DEAD

Years Ago... The Mornings After

I remember...
Washing off the stickiness
Clutching at unfamiliar bedsheets
Wondering why I couldn't manage to stay awake
Why you never helped me
Why my memory escapes me
To this day everything is shrouded in foggy capsules only you
can open
And you never have,
never do...
never will?

Where were you when I needed you?

Smart-mouthed and scathing for every little thing; but when it
mattered most, no words would come
Not 'stop', not 'no', not 'you monster...fuck off!'
An amuse bouche in a pretty face, forever marred by pain and
hate
For nothing it invited but being out of place
I should take you out...
somewhere high

Where you can see the night sky and heed gravity's call to
become one with the concrete…

Maybe then you'll shut up the voices that speak and learn to let
go by really letting go
Maybe then, you'll manage to unravel the razor cords from your
uterus
The ones that tell stories about powerlessness, paralysis, and
putridity.
You should slip into the welcoming waters and float away in
pieces, but in peace
Let the fragments evaporate
Let the memories dissipate
Happiness beckons…

Take your power back from the fragments of memory
Extricate it from the deluge of thoughts that often drive you
insane and lead you straight into the depths of needless shame
'Eediat! Why you neva fight her? Why you neva bite him?
Or run weh? Or cry? You never even tried…'
You just sat there, stood there, lay there
Clothed in worthlessness and fear
Eyes closed with bated breath, listening, waiting, feeling, woozy
Teetering off the cliff and knowing it's gone too far, but having
no strength to turn it all back and every touch stings
And you are confused because desire meets shame and your
brain says…

'Wait, this feels wrong… I'm only eight'

You want your head to say 'come on legs, we have to tell

HARD GAL FI DEAD

someone… let's make a run for it. Go! Now!'
But nothing happens
It's a funny thing when your body betrays you by responding so
well to a touch it hates
Aching for a drug that drains it, shuts it down, kills it
A blitzkrieg is coming – prepare for war
Unplug the veins… but wait, it's too late… false alarm… maybe
we misread the signs
Like we did before that time when you were nine and you told us
to run, but we thought you were fine and enjoying 'play time',
and by the time you saw the knife it was already done and the
flood was coming and the sunlight didn't come
You turned against me when I did hunger and thirst for salvation
in the forest…
On the side of the road when I reeled and hacked 'til it all
turned to black
And I woke up peeling mud, grass, dead insects from my flesh

So, tell me, where were you, when I needed you?
And why the fuck didn't you come?

Ode to a Friend Lost

Saturday, April 12, 2014 – the 'backstory'

Skeptical though I was in the months leading up to our energetic convergence, I managed to open my mind enough to go. I had already declined several invitations and referral meetings, and was in fact quite cynical about meeting some random, enlightened and erudite 'geezer' everyone referred to as 'The Guru', according to the picture I had in my head, at least; luckily, it was not so. It was a very dark time for me - something that had, unfortunately, over the years become more familiar than distant - so rather than the occasional tête-à-tête with depression, I had more bouts of dealing with it – being emotionally crippled and physically drained – than actually living my life and loving it. I was angry and sad mostly, and when I wasn't, I lived in a fog that was thick enough to shroud me, allowing me to stay far removed from everything else, (but not too thick to allow everyone around me to see and interact with the pseudo-self I presented), without suspecting much of anything. I was torn about many things and it felt like I was leaking in my spirit, but I was too vacant to stop the bleeding. Seeing, feeling, knowing and examining the gaping wound but being unable to cauterise it; I was okay with just letting it run. There wasn't much outside of that.

Autopilot days in work mode, being fake pleasant and functional, doing a job I loved doing in a place in which I loathed being. . . it drained my energy. All this, woven into a level of stress so deep, it drove me to near psychosis, near death and near to the complete loss of my essence. Sure, there were moments when I caught a glimpse of my old self, smiling, and could almost touch her, but I was never able to. In my head, I had neither time nor desire to share this willingly with anyone. In my heart, I knew I had to do it, so I did.

The Meeting…

The olive branch was extended again, and I took it, only to swiftly be hauled up out of the abyss, over hot coals and sharp stones, through the muck to end up naked on a stranger's floor, writhing in pain and screaming for help. Help that is usually promised, attempted, even, but never really comes. I was desperately hoping it would be my lucky break; so we met, and so it was. That was 482 days ago. Brief, in the traditional sense of a friendship, yet deep; in the energetic, metaphysical, timeless sense of a soulmate and friend. Our humour aligned immediately. I've always hated the word therapist. I have a way of breaking words into syllables that, given my history, made this particular one unpleasant. On that day as I dragged myself across the porch, sat on the stereotypical couch across from him and gazed around at the view…waiting, his first words at once disarmed me a little and alerted me to the fact that kinship was afoot. "So you're here to see The Rapist (therapist)… well, fuck it. I am he."

In that moment, on Saturday, April 12, 2014, I knew it would be the first truly helpful counselling experience I'd ever had. There began the most effective depression and anxiety analysis and management strategy sessions…and with it, one of the deepest friendships I've had in my life.

The Relationship…

We bonded over a shared love of science (particularly quantum physics), and music. Despite the age chasm, we had several things in common straight off the bat; both being foul-mouthed with a graphic, twisted sense of humour (we endearingly referred to each other as whoring sodomites – an inside joke about quarrelling prostitutes that had little to do with either of our actual lifestyles), having emotionally jarring experiences in our youth, and a zest for knowledge about the body and brain. He tapped into my little-known obsession with science to teach me how to really understand my afflictions, so that together we could figure out the telltale signs at the onset and I'd be better able to identify my triggers before spiraling. This man - my 'therapist' and friend - is the person I credit for helping me to the point where I could manage to go for six months straight (Dec 2014-June 2015) without sinking; after a 10-year battle with persistent depression and anxiety. I am eternally grateful to him for this.

Empathic as I am, I started feeling his death three days before it actually happened - last Wednesday - and reached out to Uncle George to take me to him before the final hour, but it was already too late. Robby, or 'The Guru' as some called him, wore many hats as life coach/neuro-linguistic therapist to many, former pilot, singer/songwriter and founding member of the band 'Chalice'… amongst others.

The Denouement…

Myriad thoughts and nonplussed half-feelings are running through me at the moment. I've been so apathetic in the past month that I'm yet to really react or respond to the news of his death. I also completely missed his thanksgiving service yesterday. At the forefront is a feeling of being cheated of my chance to really say goodbye and having no one to blame but myself. I wonder what would happen if I'd tried to extract my head from my own ass and been there more as his friend in the final lap; if it would have made any difference? Would he be sure then, how much I cared for him? Understand, that I retreated because he would know I was slipping and I didn't want that as an additional burden? On the other hand, I know I did all I could, when I could. From the constant phone calls to showing up at the hospital with food he actually wanted to eat, and an irreverent joke here and there. If anything, there's one thing I do owe him – the proof that I'm really taking his advice.

"Tami, stop letting fear consume you."

"Stop hiding your light from the world – you are amazing and magnificent, you have something significant to offer to the world and that's why you're so magnetic. There's a reason why people gravitate to you all the time. Get over it."

"Where the fuck is your confidence child? Raasclaat man! Sometimes I really want to land you a swift kick in the head."

"Why are you choosing to be cynical and angry? It's a mask. Stop holding on to it, you're a lover _and_ a fighter… we both know that."

"I only want the best for you and I need you to understand that you must also want that for yourself."

Only this time, I will say I agree with you and actually mean it. Walk good, sodomite.

Volume III

Sisters of My Song: The Lessons

Lesson 1
War Paint

I've been struggling with depression for years. In fact my earliest memory of the ominous, fatigued, self-deprecating feelings it brings was at eight years old - the year I wrote my first suicide note - although back then, I didn't even fully understand what it was that I did. I just knew the thoughts I had, eating me... and was led to put them on paper.

I'm still doing the rounds in this ring. The battle to maintain equilibrium over the years has been far from easy; I've had to employ and create new strategies to stay on top of it. Like when I'm hanging off the edge and can see no other option but to clock out, I pull out my paints and make-up, spread them all about me and put on my 'war paint' as a reminder that my story is still being written.

I am not defeated and will not be defeated as long as there are still beautiful things - like art - to focus on and look forward to.

Lesson 2
Too Pretty/Through The Tears

Hello, beautiful (he looks me up and down)... Are you here for visitation? If so, you're a bit late. I can't even see what I can do for you at this point.

No, I'm not. I'm collecting medication.

Oh! (Pause) Come this way.

(I step into the brightly lit passage and he now sees that I've clearly been crying for years)

What's the matter, dear?

I just told you, medicine, please. I need it. (I follow him into the office)

Doctor, nurse, this young lady needs some meds... I think she's very depressed.

(The doctor turns around) I'll be right with you Miss?

Coley.

Right, Miss Coley. Have a seat here, nurse will take your vitals while you wait.

(She takes over) Any diagnosed mental illnesses, Miss Coley?

Yes. A few.

Okay, fill this out, please.
(I do so in-between silent rivers incessantly flowing down my
face. The doctor comes over and sits with me, she leaves. He
asks me a bunch of seemingly innocent, unrelated questions. I
respond on autopilot, feeling nothing, until he says...)

I'm sorry, Miss Coley, but we can't just medicate you,
especially with your current mindset. For us to treat you, you'll
have to be admitted. Nurse, take her around to the female
ward, please.

(Male nurse from earlier walks in and my fire returns for a
second)

Wtf? No! I can't do that. I am not staying here. I came here
to get help!

And we are going to help you. Don't worry, it's only until you
stabilise and you will be fine. We are concerned for your safety,
so since you live alone, we cannot allow you to leave unless we
release you into the care of a family member. It's our policy. (He
talks to the nurse) Please call the ward and take her around.

Me: Don't touch me! I am fine. I just need the damn
medicine. If I really wanted to die, I wouldn't be here. This is
bullshit!

(He's clearly used to it and continues to ignore my protests
while he escorts me around. The doctor is already gone and I'm
too drained to continue)

Nurse: Shame... you're way too pretty to be in a place like

33

this, or to be depressed all the time. When they let you out, make sure you change your diet and start exercising every day.

If you have a boyfriend, get him to work out with you. It's free medicine.

Me, dryly: Yeah, that's great. Thanks. I'll be out in the morning, right?

(He shrugs) Who knows? You'll be out whenever we can trust you not to do it.

Lesson 3
Ward Welcome/A Friendly Tip

(I walk into the ward behind the nurse, still crying. Terrified, tense... A young nurse greets me.)

Welcome, Miss Coley. Don't look so sad and frightened. We won't hurt you here and it's not the end of the world. And don't think you're above this either. We treat everyone. From lawyers, doctors, college students and politicians to beauty queens like yourself. A former Miss Jamaica was in here just last week. You'll be fine. Please sign in all your personal belongings, you can't take anything with you beyond this point. You also get one phone call, since you were not supposed to stay here tonight.
It says here you have been awake for almost two weeks now. Do you know who you need to call or would you like to sleep first?

Yes.

Yes what? Phone call or sleep?

Phone call, please. I'm not tired.

You sure? You need to sleep. How long now you crying?

I'm sure. I'm not really crying. I just can't turn the tears off.

Hmph. Okay, here's the phone, you have three minutes. You're on bed #2, it's right there where we can see you.

(I make my phone call then walk over to the bed, look around and think of my days in boarding school. It all looks oddly familiar. She continues, louder...)

Is bedtime now, Miss Coley. At least lie down. Try sleep. You can't stand there all night.

(A different nurse comes over. She's older, with a kind energy. I can tell she's worked there a long time)

Miss Coley?

Yes, nurse?

Did you tell the doctor about your suicidal thoughts?

Yes, I did.

That's why you're here. That, with the non-stop crying. If you want to get out of here quick, you must stop the crying and make sure you convince them that you not thinking to kill yourself anymore. And make sure you call a family member with them head screw on to come sign you out. Alright? I have to leave now. I'll come check on you in the morning.

Okay, thanks a lot.

Never mind, lie down. You soul tired. You just don't know it yet.

Lesson 4 – Kindred

Hey new girl, why are you here?
Depression, or bi-polar, right?

Yes. That's right. How did you know?

Lucky guess. (She laughs)
You're like me… a misfit.
Not quite right in the head, but not as crazy as the rest.
I'm actually a law student.
By the way, if you're not going to sleep, may I use your sheet?
It's chilly, but they won't give me one.

Why not?
Oh. They're afraid I'll hang myself.

Lesson 5- My life Was Stolen
Hello, me neighbour. My name is Myrtle.

Good night, Miss Myrtle.

I dunno why them put me in here. Like me live on bed #3,
me have a house, you know?
My own house I work hard to build. I live there with my son.

Oh, that's nice. Where is that?

Me not telling! Everybody want to *tief* it. Family is not a
good thing. Them throw me out, you know? Run out my son out of
me own yard. Me work hard for it. By myself. Just me and me son.
No father. Them kill him father, so is just me and him. Years me live
there. And them run we!
Me son never tek it well at all, him was too young for the stress.

I'm sorry to hear that, Miss Myrtle, where is he now?

Where is he? Him dead!!! Them kill him off! And dem tek weh
me house and leave me a road!
Ohhhhhhhhhh my son... my son... Kevin!!! Oh... my son!
(She gets much louder)
Me want me house! Gimme back me house!
Gimme back me son! Why you kill off me son?
Gimme back me life!
'Bout family... me hate all a dem!
Whoooooy...

Nurse: Myrtle, shut up! You going wake up everybody!

Kindred: I should have warned you, you know. Now she's

going to go on all night
Lesson 6 - Banshee

Who is she?
Gliding by… moaning
Lithe, graceful, eerie
Tickles your feet, ever so softly while you sleep
Bringing the chill, she grabs off your 'blankie'
And squeals with delight - jumps back in fright as you twitch
She ducks behind your bed, shaking the floor
Sending bottles and jars in an untidy spread
She flits around until morning comes
Then you look over your shoulders and you see her
She says, 'Don't look at me… you evil!'

Lesson 7
Bourgeoisie

Nurse:
Alright ladies, time to wake up! Good morning. Get ready to
shower and start the day. Let's go! Janet, you're not moving.
Chop-chop.

Janet: (Hisses) How many times do I have to tell you? I am not a
morning person. That's why I went into business for myself. Made
my own hours. I don't do this shit! (She turns to look at me)

What is it, new girl? I am an accountant, an excellent one, too!
I've worked all over the world and made lots of money. Flown first
class. Shopped in all the best stores. You think I'm stupid like

these others? I'm not even supposed to be here... I'm just bi-polar.

(She walks off to the shared closet and picks up what looks like a trench coat)

Nurse: Where you going in that, Janet? You want to *bun up* in here today?
(She turns to me) Coley, you can get something from the closet to wear until your own clothes come. Pick out something to wear.

Janet, shrieking: You feisty, nurse! This is a fucking Gucci coat!!! I bought this in Italy!

Nurse: Impressive. Now get in the shower, Janet. I'm not playing with you today.

Lesson 8 – Truck

Vrooooom! Bi-beep-beep! Urkssss!
Hi Miss, what a nice day!
Just drink a nice cuppa tea, yes man!
You like tea? Me love tea.
But these ladies in here. . . unruly
Dem don't really like me.
I am too positive for this place.
I have to elevate myself from these women
Yes, man!
All of them... Their mind messed up. Dem stressed!
But not me you know,
I am a truck.

Lesson 9 – Mary-Ann

Pretty little girl, what's your name?

My name is Mary-Ann.
I love to skip-hop-jump as high as a plane
But, no matter what... I still end up, here.
I don't know why, but I know why.
Maybe I'm lonely.
My baby son, he died.
I hate it here. It's not so nice but
The doctors say I have 'kitopreenia', so it's my only chance of
having a good life
Life is different outside.
In here I have a home and some friends, it's not so cold as
outside.
No one understands me there.
But, in here, at least I know when I'm alive and I can behave
myself,
I don't have to try.
What was your name again, my dear?
Are you going to eat that?
Do you like it in here?

Lesson 10
Fire Mumma/Beg Yuh Some

Pretty girl! How you reach in here?

I'm bi-polar and suicidal, so they apparently think it's not safe for
me to go home.

Oh yeah? Alright then. (Pause) You remind me of my sister.

Is her name (I call her sister's name)?

Yeah man, you know her? How you know her?

Yes, I do. She's cool. I've heard that we look alike before, too. She's a model. I'm a make-up artist. We're in the same circles.

Oh, cool. I'm a model too, you know, but I'm younger. Maybe we can do a shoot together one day.

Sure. You definitely look like a model for real. So… why are you here?

(She laughs, shyly) Thanks. Psychosis dem say, but it's really because I'm always trying to burn down my house.

Wtf? Why?

Spirits. Demons. Everything in there… Nobody believes me and I am NOT staying in there with them. That's for sure. So you still do make-up?

Sometimes, but not that much any more.

What you into now?

Well I'm writing a book and it's almost done.

That's nice. Make sure you put me in it and make sure you finish it, too.

Okay, I will. You're very interesting.

Yes… so make sure you visit me when you leave here, too.

You don't plan to get out?

Yeah man, but it's my third time now. I will probably come back. Where you got that food from by the way? It look nice.

My sister Sim sent it over. She wants me to start eating again.

Oh, she works here?

Nah. She used to. She's in Bermuda now.

So how she send the food?

She ordered it on the phone and sent it to her friend who still works here. Her friend took it to me.

Must be love. (She laughs) But since you nah really eat it, beg you some nuh?

Sure. Knock yourself out. I don't have an appetite.

Ahhhh… pass it here. You a good youth… I will share it up. We soon get some meds man. After that, you will get your appetite back and you will sleep, too. Take care, new friend.

Lesson 11
Bethelda

Nurseeeeeee!!!! Nurseeeeee!!! Nurseeeee!!! Help me!

Nurse: Hi, hello! Not today again with the noise! Sit down and keep quiet Bethelda!

(She grabs her dress off and rips it down the middle. Pulls off her underwear and lies down on the floor, naked, screaming for help. The nurses all continue to ignore her. She then rolls herself like a barrel out of the ward, through and into the corridor, still naked. Still screaming. Again, no one bats an eyelid. Some time passes and the screams turn into wails, then into moaning. Then she goes silent. I walk outside to see what's happening and a nurse follows suit).

Nurse: Coley, leave Bethelda alone. She alright. She soon calm down. (She picks her clothes up and goes over to her with them) How much clothes you plan to tear up miss?

Bethelda: Don't want no clothes! My pussy don't like panty. Panty burn me! Leave me alone.
(She then contorts herself into an odd position on the wall, still seated on the ground)

Nurse: Come man, you don't want some food? It's soon lunch time.

(She gives her a blank stare and has clearly already travelled off somewhere in her mind. The nurse tries to fix her arms, but her limbs are stiff and immoveable. I'm standing there confounded.)

Nurse: She alright man. We just have to leave her for a little while. I was trying to get her to eat and take the pills before this happen, but it's earlier than usual today.

So you're not going to move her back inside? She is all bent up and naked.

Nurse: Who? Me? No sah! You see how she heavy? She will be alright. She's just catatonic, among many other things.

(The kind nurse from last night shouts my name from the inside, I walk back in towards her)

Come, Miss Coley, here's some water… it's time for your meds.

Sneak Peek Inside My Mind

Things to do this week...

Love myself more – and honour my temple in all ways
Get some rest
Drink more water
Eat some damn food (and on time, for fuck's sake)
Do some form of exercise... or try yoga (both?)
Try to relax every day (at least once)
Start reconnecting (with self x people – especially family and friends)
Get shit done!

Fathers' Day?

I've always hated it. I'm 29 and as much as it makes more sense to me, I don't love it now, either, because growing up, I had everything I needed but that. It was the thing I envied everyone else for, because mine denied me publicly, like Peter. It was the only thing I couldn't disprove by debating or excelling at.

No matter what I did, he didn't want anything to do with me, or my Mum, like other kids' parents did.

I could do nothing to stop the hurt, the frustration, the emptiness, the jealousy, the longing and not belonging – it coloured everything - and I believe in some way, that it still does.

That's probably where all the anger, detachment and aggression comes from... still, there's hope.

He's now digressed, and I'm a lot less ascetic as I've aged, but the damage is still pretty bad.

Although I have forgiven him, I'm not sure that it's something you ever really get over.

Especially so brutally done.

Or is it?

On Presence...

As a child, I did not know my father. I knew who he was, his name, his car, what he looked like, what he did for a living, who he dated. All data. There was no real presence of him in my life. My parents never spoke a word to each other since about a month or two after I entered this plane of existence and I loathed him, especially. I thought he was the most disconnected, arrogant asshole I'd ever met, and was in fact happy we weren't closer, so I'd have to learn how to deal with him.

It's a very long and complex story, one that made my childhood heavy, despite having my amazing grandfather, 'Daddy', and a team of AMAZING uncles who stepped up, loved and fathered me brilliantly. I lacked nothing and had a bunch of shit I didn't really care about. I knew without a doubt that I was loved. Still, while hating him in my childlike mind, I wondered what I could possibly have done as a baby to make him hate me first. There was always this hole, you see, because no matter what, fathers matter. Especially to their children.

I carried that question in my heart for years and it made me angry, bitter, bitchy and cruel, especially to men. And it took a long time for me to put the pieces together. It took a long time for me to accept his need to reconnect, and not snub him, and listen.

I was 25 when I figured it out, confronted the darkness within myself and started letting him back in.

We're now writing a new story.

Things are different; better, it's a work in progress.

I say all this to say that, if you ever have the chance to be a father, <u>be one</u> and remember, it also includes loving and respecting the mother. Children see, feel, know and understand everything, and your behaviour teaches them more than you know.

On 'Getting Help'

Therapy is really helping me. As much as I fought it, I'm glad I went. In fact, I'd go every week if I could afford it. Maybe even twice (because, let's face it, I need that shit).

She's great, oddly comforting to speak with. She's given me a lot of practical tips and is very good at helping me analyse and realise my thoughts and emotions. I can also see where I'm already putting it to good use – especially when I start to spiral. I never thought I'd say this, but at this point in my development, it's just what I need. I wish there wasn't such a stigma, because I really feel more people should know that and benefit from it.

Maybe that's why I'm here...

Modern Woman

Eschew all notions of meek submissiveness by acquiescing to a man's every request or need.
Today, gender roles are promptly deconstructed.
Dare to question, unlearn even, everything you once knew.
Enter the independent Alpha Female, the lady boss, the goal digger who will not be held back by labels and expectations.
Gone are the days of women waiting around to be married and carried off into the sunset to live barefoot and pregnant, happily ever after.
Today's woman is the dream chaser who yearns to earn, learn, travel, vote, drive, shop, live, raise her family...on her own terms.
Her ideal mate is one who strongly supports her endeavours, nurtures her passion, understands her power and is man enough to let his ego take a back seat when needed.
He allows her to step forward, vibrate higher and shine...
Without being threatened by her divine feminine energy.

2017 Feels

In December of 2016, after a very rough and tumultuous end to the year, or rather to the last three (to five years); I said 2017 was mine. Today I'm reflecting on the events that have shaped my life since and the feelings that linger as a result. Death, a car accident, conflicts, work, strained relationships, mental health issues, lack of balance, respite, belonging and real 'grounded-ness'.

As much as these things have helped me grow and come more into who and what I am, they also make me question everything. I've never been more confused and unsure-footed.

On one hand things are looking up, and on the other, spiraling and overflowing.

I'm at once the detached observer, the one puzzle piece that doesn't fit and the overburdened, too-invested nuisance who can't figure out how to unplug from the matrix.

Asking every day, who am I? Where am I going? What am I doing?

What do I even want to do? And, watching the answer change each day.

It is a strange, difficult and interesting time-space-reality to be in.

Who has answers, anyway?

Life, as we all know, is in the questions.

Poems…

Rock x Release

Pick up your problems
Head to the sea
Toss in your issues
Stand there... just be
It's about perspective
The vista will show
There's something much greater
Learn
Absorb
Grow.

Ra: God of the Sun

Slow... rising tremor
Roar... quickening beat
Drums like dub, beating
Waiting, awakening, pulsating
A tinkle of cymbals
The clamour of bells
Shards of light reach out
Tickle the grass
Snake 'cross the rooftops
Roll back the fog
Zephyrs kiss the mountains
Drinking in beads of sweat
Sprung up overnight as whispering leaves bear witness
Fresh petals unfold in worship
Anxious crickets make their beds
Ushering in terror... stillness, hush
Golden shards pierce the land
Unleashing his fury into the cracks
Ant caravans march out from their lair
Roosters, hens... flutter in fear
Shining river, screaming waves
Comforting chaos
Mother Earth in praise for when he comes
As he comes... it is morning.

Tropical Punaani

You.
Shining with the sun
Shimmering like the sea
Rough and inviting
Dangerous, exciting
You.
Wid you wiya waist
Curls, coils, kinks
Choke cherry links
Rotten history inked
You.
With di backside
Full of jokes and rhythm
You gumption like rum
Resilient like red dirt stain
You.
Smell like a fresh Julie mango
Fleshy, inviting lips
Just ripe, wid di right amount of sweet
And your teeth, lovely teeth woyoiii...
You.
Mesmerise me like the crown of the pine
And you just as sharp
With you back broad like ship deck
And you warm heart, fiery tongue
You.

Tropical
Punaani,
Mystical
You.
Black woman
Red woman
Moon woman
Hold the key, shoulder them secrets
Hear you whisper it like bamboo bush
Until you forget
Your mother never tell you
She forget too
If sugar cane could talk
To cotton tree
They would tell your granny
To tell me, to tell you
That the same sky bring dark cloud
Hailstone and rain
Bring cerulean hopes
And music, friendship... bliss
Temporary salve for the pain
Ask your other grandmother
She know, too
The sweetness and thickness of your flesh
The magic and terror it holds
The taste of freedom and old sin
Little wonder, my dear
You walk on tiny needles in your shoes
Thanking generations of tightrope walkers before you
For their balancing skill
Their moxy and will
Fret not your soul, Queen
Press not your hair
Don't forget your story

HARD GAL FI DEAD

You tread lightly on the earth, but your essence remains pungent
Womb-man
Soft, strong, beautiful
You are so much more than enough.

Death by Frankincense

Dark, heady... sweet and strong
At once kind and comforting
Just enough to feed you warmth
Playful, enveloping
Blue Mountain Coffee rich
Like thorns - wild, sharp and dangerous
Distinctly fragrant
Waxing wise - deep... vast
Mesmerising like the sky on a pristine day
Right after the rain when
The clouds have cleared and the air is clean
At the right time, and it's just what you need to jar you, refresh
you
Just like the sea peels back from the shore
A presence you feel, a confidence you know
Like a candle, fading... yet ever so bright
Vulnerable, fighting
Leaning into blackness that only you can taste
As it beckons and pulls
Wafting above you, dancing around you
Creeping up on you
Cradles and rocks you
Roaming and ready to snake around your neck
Touching you ever so gently
Tightening, loosening, winning, smiling
Oscillating, undulating...
Into the light.

Insomnia

One day
I will sink into you
Sweetly
Softly
Unreservedly
Smile as you engulf me
Finally
You will elude me no more
And say
Welcome home.

Advocate

I open doors and aim at closing wounds
Illuminate bruises long hidden and say, 'now, show me yours'
Bare my soul to the world
Hoping this quivering fire still gets me across borders
Into heads and hearts and ears so
I can change the world, one mind at a time
And, yet…
In my own house
Words boomerang against sepulchre stones
Roll away
And fall flat against my feet, mocking me.

Coward

You say I'm emotional... it's true
I find no shame or weakness in that
I bare my soul. It's who I am
I am committed, loyal, passionate; I love fiercely. I don't cheat
I can be a bit naïve and slow to act, but stupid, I am not

Look me in the eyes, handsome devil, while you throw empty
words around
Be convincing for once. Tell me what's really going on,
instead of discrediting my intuition with words like 'suspicious',
'untrusting', 'over-thinker' and 'insecure'
Before serving up spiels of lies, omissions, mind games and re-
frames
Peppered with lines, well-crafted, you think, but they fall flat
before my spirit
'You just won't give me the benefit of the doubt'
'Stop looking for reasons why we won't work out, because you're
afraid of love'
'Be completely open, throw yourself under the bus'
'These kinds of questions are just you holding us back'
'She's lying'
'I am not your ex'
'Stop making me walk on eggshells'
'We're just friends, she just has no one else to turn to'
'I can't control the behaviour of other women';
'I am not flirting, I'm just a charming man'

HARD GAL FI DEAD

'She came on to me first'

'I gave in because you were away and I missed you'
'I wanted to explore what I felt to understand it more but I think I regret it now'
'Your depression doesn't scare me, I want to understand it, I'm here for you'

What do you know about love, love?
Nothing
For love is kind
Don't dish out selfishness, pain, inconsideration, disrespect
Then turn around and call me emotional or insecure
Don't tell others I'm 'just crazy', or 'she listens to everyone else but the man she's with'
Own your shit if you can dish it
If you must broadcast what was once ours
Let them know that when I 'just got up one day and left'
I'd not taken leave of my senses, as you made it seem, but rather regained them,
That I'd simply decided I'd had enough
When you were out making me look like a fool, you were unconcerned, proud
Busy 'just talking', 'networking and making friends'
Don't hide now behind the façade of my mental health journey
Be just as brave to show everyone the shitty hand you dealt

Single

This is new
I'm alone and… okay
Not lonely, not scorned
In solitude
At peace
No tug-of-war with the sheets
No 'side of the bed'
No walking on eggshells
Exhausting commotions
Five-day arguments
I go where I will
I eat, watch and do what I want
It's lovely, and I enjoy it
Do I miss you? Hardly
What I really missed was myself, but
She's back and now we're having fun
Reconnecting
Earthing
Solo dance parties
Elaborate meals
Naked yoga with candles, beach sounds and soothing smells
Writing out torment from our weathered essence
Manifesting new dreams
'Yasssssssss - queen-ing'
Blowing smoke up each other's asses
Your presence is missing, yes,
But I'm surviving

Hell, thriving
Re-aligning
Learning again to love for me
To love my own company
Who is this awesome woman?
This bubbly, child-like girl?
Confident, glowing, sexy...
No toxic actions
No second-guessing her words
I like her. I love her
I'll remember next time to keep her around

As it unfolds

I
I see stars in his eyes
A spring in his step and
I know how safety feels in his arms
Such a pity he doesn't see
His existence reminds me of you...

II
We humans are so complex
How interesting it is to seek solace
In the welcoming arms of an uncommitted soul
Knowing that each rendezvous
Widens the gap just a little bit more.

III
Your 'I love you's' fall on deaf ears
And yet
My breath quickens at your touch
My thoughts recoil, gently
My stomach curls up in sadness and shame
For I know now, that it isn't you
And never will be.

IV
The song and dance of futility
Lies beside us in our bed

I hear my overworked heart scream, 'You must leave him!'
And thoughts behind the ceiling I've come to know so well
Continue to taunt me …

V
For what is hope but to give a little more?
Close your eyes and connect with
the potential that hides within?
Forsaking all other signs
To accept this moment
Knowing the stars in his eyes are embers of a fire
Long burning for someone else

Taken

Nerves on high
Breaths all shallow
I twitch
You stare...
You pull
I swallow
Weeks of reasoning
Yesses, noes,
Conversations flow
Too well, it seems
No time to think
Relax, react
Taste the way
Passions blaze up
In the castles of our skin
Touch, sweat... Hearts drum the same rhythm
Shoulders, back
Locks unravel
Arms, navels
Fingers entwine
Nipples, knees
Kisses all over
Sharp breaths
Sweet release, calming rain

HARD GAL FI DEAD

Too late, we know
Laughter and then…
Us… Finally.
Tangled in this web
Crack a smile and with another kiss, we sin again

Unborn

Things could have turned out differently if we'd met
How? I don't know
I sometimes consider not cutting you out, but
I would still say 'no'
I was just a girl
Physically surrounded, emotionally alone
You might not understand this but, though I loved you, I have no
regrets
I treasured the moments we had to ourselves
When I wondered who and how you'd be
When our bodies were one
No mother should have to bury her child
I didn't even get to say goodbye
You were part of me when you felt my fears and my decision
And it hurt
Five years I grieved you in a cloud
Dark
Empty
Wearing human bandages for respite
Until I accepted my actions and forgave them all
I want you to know, son,
You were created in love and so, too, released.
For once
Self-love was chosen to reign over everything
And a new understanding was born
That our energies, our souls, are forever embraced
Visit it in the realms and know

Enter The Corridors

I answered the call
I did, and my eyes gleamed with wonder
Down the corridors
I skipped past the lockers
My teaspoon of freedom no match for the rapids ahead of me
I was so trusting; I forgot I never learned how to swim
I came in with cavernous insides – hollow
Self-inflicted wounds of all kinds, months old
Hearing screams in my mind of my lost child
Going a bit crazy, heartfelt
Entering a new world of darkness I'd never seen
Love, betrayal, judgment I'd never felt
Alone
Despondent
Numb
Yes, five long years of growth and torment

Phoenix Flight

It's dark in my heart
Worse, inside my mind
I have stoned and been stoned
Crumbled and cracked
Dazed and abandoned
Used and denied
Then wake up and use my bare hands
to pull swords lodged deep into my head
Out into light and then bandage my hands
Lick my wounds in astonishment
For I am yet to fall… how?
Many left me for dead, some are already long gone
Others are only here for themselves, to drain me
Then rejoice of their own renewed health
Until the hour comes when I will burst into flames
Grow wings and say…fuck you, what about me?

Pickney, borne of Joy

I feel her in the back of my neck
Like the sun, merciless, beating down on me
Hot and sticky, holding my breath
I see her
Writhing, swearing on the ground as she plucks the sword of
discrimination from her side

Foaming at the mouth... only diffidence remains
Self-esteem long carted away on a gust of wind
Dislodging the thorns around her head
Leaving demons inside her head to shriek
No love, no sleep, no place to belong
Darkness, her violent lover
Doubt, misery, paranoia, her friends

How does it feel to embrace your sins?
Carry them faithfully on your back for miles and years
Wear them boldly on your forehead
Wipe them away as they leak through your eyes
Plug them with scriptures as they flow from your chest, Staining
everything?

When inadequacy colours your very soul
And pain and shame stand together in your belly
How does it feel to be here, but not?
To be surrounded, yet lonelier than you've ever been?

HARD GAL FI DEAD

Trust, a precious gem, stolen from your childish hands in deep
slumber
Nothing else matters or makes sense
Not even you, not even me, or we...

They are all there to judge you
Exploit you
Take your innocent acceptance
Twist your view of the world
Leave you dry and call you slut
'Wotless' and lazy follow suit
'Chupid', 'nasty dog'...

Embarrassing, they say
Where's the help when you need it?
Or worse yet, how do you know where to seek it?
And when?
What use is connection when everyone whips and leaves you?
If not in body, in heart and mind
With words that back you into a corner
Build a fence around you
Separates you from the real world
Forcing you, the life of the party
The ultimate social butterfly, the charming and charitable to
become
Misunderstood, reticent, shelved
Alone

Joy is your name, and yet nothing eludes you more
I am welcomed into your world of sadness
Days knitted into each other, holding no substance

HARD GAL FI DEAD

I emerge from this pool of bitterness between your thighs
As you sing of lost love
To swim through icy waters
Navigate jagged terrain
Climb over hot stones and fall at your feet, begging
For a love you're not sure you have
And wake up to tell you this…
We are each other
With the strength of a thousand horses trotting in our veins
We are wombmen, left for dead
Now rising together to claw away the earth piled upon us
Building homes from our crosses' logs
Exhausted, but always charging on.

Farewell, Angel

(For Christopher Joseph Miguel Soutar II – Aug 1, 2009 – Oct 8, 2011)

You made us laugh, cry, marvel at you
Your bright eyes always seemed to spell truth
You made a lasting impression everywhere you went
Your vibrant energy, sincerity, comforting nature always felt
Sweet, innocent, wise beyond your years
Adventurous too, you showed no fear
We all wished so much to see you grow
Be the best you could be, warm our hearts with the love you'd
always show
Your unexpected departure, we'll never comprehend
Such a deep-seated wound seems unable to mend
We'll miss you terribly, Baby Chris, our sweet angel
and never stop loving you…

Hey there, Little Sis!

Hey there, little sis!
You are so beauty-FULL
Full of laughs, jokes and fire
Questioning everything
Neverland rhythm
Smart, different, entertaining

Vividly etched in my memory, your first day of school
I remember the little smile
Your little hands gripping your umbrella and lunchbox
Eyes wide
Socks to your knees
Ready for a new adventure
How you love poetry, music and Spanish
How you struggled with making real friends
You loved to wake up and get ready for the day
Excited to learn and be outside
So much joy, so much promise
So much love for others

Be not afraid or discouraged
By the things that burn
The piercing stigma
And tumultuous, unexpected, sharp turns
The changed, now restrictive course

HARD GAL FI DEAD

Harsh words, medicinal haze, grinding halt

Your intelligence remains
Your beauty? Still there
Creativity, curiosity
Ability to learn and grow, untamed

So much has changed about you
And yet so little has
Life can still be beauty-FULL
It is and will be - changes do happen

I see it, I see you
Excelling
Fulfilling
Exciting
Successful
Understanding yourself
Your life
Your power and purpose
Though the rest stop is quite long
Your journey isn't over yet, my love
Little sis, you have much to give
And a beauty-FULL life filled with love and meaning to live.

Welcome Back

Welcome back, little brother
I love you still… I never stopped
Carried you in my heart
Always within

Welcome back, little brother
I hope you felt the hole we plugged
When we found out you left

Welcome back, little brother
I missed your big smile
Your eyes, so kind
Your spirit, so wild

Your hugs, so warm
Your presence, so strong
Energy so great
I'd love to catch up, it's never too late

Welcome back, little brother
Though you're now a man
Returning to us from a dark, twisted land
I wish you well
I hope you've grown

Heed the ugly lessons and see

HARD GAL FI DEAD

That everything is a choice
And every hand we are dealt
Every ounce of pain we feel in life
Is for our evolution into our highest state of being

Welcome back, little brother
Things have changed so much
For you
In you
Around you
About you
But
In all of this, remember, you are still you
Your 'you-ness' remains
You are changed, but yet… unchanged

Be great, be free
Be grateful for freedom
Thankful for your support system, family is everything

Regret and remorse will come but
Remember to forgive
And start the forgiveness with yourself
You deserve it
You are still a king
For everyone, life is a series of tests and lessons
Try to learn them once and move forward
Upward and onward in love and newfound appreciation for the
world

It is still so wonderful, even with all the darkness within it
It will be extremely tough, no doubt, little brother…
But necessary
And possible.

Empath (Beware The News)

Words impale my skin like a sharpened stake
Specially carved for my chest
Searing into my Motherland flesh
It stings my eyes – the images
Tear into my psyche
Letting in the reality of my dark… skin
And the cold, the fear and hopelessness
Melancholia takes root, yes
It strangles me slowly
Burns through my chest… and I shriek
Sounds run down my face into red pools at my feet
Planted firmly in the fields as I weep
Stepping back in my head
Counting bodies in the street.

Self.Soul.Surgery

You are tired, my dear
Your spirit needs replenishing
Cut yourself open
Pluck out the things that no longer serve you
Hold them in both hands, and
Bleed that self-doubt into the earth that supports you, still
Lower them parasites into the fire
And
Watch them erupt, dance, die
Then
Stretch forth your hands to the sky
Let your glassy eyes follow the smoke
Breathe toxicity out and know that
Evolution hurts darling, but
You're so worth it.

Rain

Wash
My eyes, my face, my heart and soul
Cleanse
My thoughts, my lips, my fears
R
i
n
s
e

a
w
a
y

d
i
s
c
o
u
r
a
g
e
m
e
n
t

Comfort disappointment
Dissolve the past and make it new
Beat down on me, pellets of wisdom
Nourish me with resolve, clarity
Silence my dubious mind, and
Quiet my fiery tongue
Take me now… inside myself
To let it all go on crisp, clean air
Gorged, clogged, cleared, clean
So I can begin renewal and change

The Rising

(for the women who've had enough)

One day your disinterest and disrespect will not matter
Your abuse and neglect will stir no response
And everyone you seek to fill the hole, boost the ego, feed the
mind
Will turn their backs and move along
Then
You will find yourself crawling back, to that 'real one'
The one who's always there...
Only your cries will fall on deaf ears
You will apologise when she's already free
Love her most when she's gone
Bleed sincerity into your sheets on those terrible nights when you
just cannot sleep
And feel the crushing weight of being alone
For she is worlds away now – over you, over there
Loving herself
And knowing she's everything.

Letters to Dead Men

Thanks for fucking off, darling
For learning all my ways
Sketching our future
All while drinking me up
Then spitting me out, like vinegar
Saying I was insufferable, too difficult, detached or depressed
With insecurities for eons
Not quite as magical as you first thought when
You plucked me
The thorn ripped through your finger, but you didn't scream
No, you smiled and laid me down, gently
So neatly, I almost fell asleep
You were long gone by the time I noticed you were right
There's no place for you here
I never made one
It was all in my head...
And you couldn't water a garden that's already dead.

Abysmal

Touched so much
You don't want to be
Not even by a gentle wind
Caressing your skin
Overlooked, so much
You learn not to be seen
Loved, so little
Scorned so vehemently
Lied to… repeatedly
So much, you can't breathe
Can't speak… won't speak
So much, you don't know
Or want to know love
Come, then… let us play.

Mama Lashy

Loving, strong, kind in heart
Knowledgeable, rooted in spirit
Sharp-tongued, Mother Supreme
God-fearing, industrious queen
She will give you her ass and shit through her ribs
Breathe through her skin
Lash you – not with belts, or fists
But arsenic words from vitriolic lips

Big you up, tear you down
Bleed your self-esteem right out
Strangle your dreams
Feed you ice cream
And a prayer for your starving heart
Weaknesses, ailments, nuances

Rebuild your broken dreams
Make you some tea, for everything
You want an icy mint? How about some porridge?
Come, drink it…

Feed you full of righteousness, scripture and truth
Dress you to the nines while the firing squad shoots
Keep you healthy, tend you strong
Tell you that you don't belong
Correct your homework, teach you to read

HARD GAL FI DEAD

Soothe your forehead with rum, your chest with Vick's
Your bedroom walls with olive oil and Holy Water
Your doorways with salt
Teach you life, shut you up
Pity you, spin you round

What's family, anyway?
The ones who raise you… prune you, make you strange
Silent, abrasive… disengaged
The self-conscious kinship, sweet turbulence in a comfort zone
The home you love, but never sleep peacefully in
It's the one you sink into… bloom out of
Question, yet connect to
Remembering love amid lashes, respect, fear and hurt
As you grow into loving yourself.

Building Blocks

Idiot! You don't hear me call you?
Open your ears and listen
Shut up your mouth! You too damn bright
Remember, you shouldn't be here.
You were a mistake
Say thank God you have everything you need – you don't live
on the street!
Better study your book and learn some sense, quick
Before you turn into a worthless vessel like the one you come
here in
You not too young to understand life, you hear me?
'Bout you want play.

Martyr

Acidity oozes from your lips
Down your chin
Into your chest
Coloured with fear and longing, betrayal and burden
Your clothes stained with freedom and fun sacrificed
Replaced with the swell of pain and youthful marriage
13 counts of childbirth – one sentence short
Money worries, judgment, not much support
Your feet have held you so long, and now, they need support

Misunderstood, some pull away
Withhold their joy, visits and aid without examining the depths of
your pain
Stress is your friend
The Father, your confidante
Exhaustion, your ageless companion
Still, you know love, because you are love

Harsh words and quick criticisms hardly hide an exceptional
heart
So big and full, you've overflowed into many lives
For those who need a helping hand – a reminder of the love of
God
You offer it without question
So fiery, so full, so nurturing
Layers of strength through decades, burn out

HARD GAL FI DEAD

Floating away on the memories of your lover
Phenomenal and formidable, yes
But you are human, too, my love.

Soar

Too many days have found me lowly
Squeezing my last breath for sustenance
Cocooned, burning quietly, fading into ashes
Finding neither hope nor sleep
And yet
A new day breaks and divine mystery with it comes
With gold light to seal the cracks
So I can take flight…

What I know

When my mind is racing and my breath is caught up
In the spaces between my mouth and throat
When feelings flow over - hot, cold, stale, fun, doubt, guilt,
shame, peace
When salty tears run through my bowels - an alternate exit
When my stomach churns, and queasiness begs, sit
When the hairs stand aligned in the back of my neck
Chest tight, ears hot, palms wet
You've always been there... my pen, my friend
So how can I not write?

My Last

You were…
My last hurrah
My final dance
Who looked behind my eyes and asked, 'is everything alright?'
You took the branch and poked around
Striking dark places
Pulling me into the sun
Acknowledging pain inside my smiles
Warmed them with care
Tempting fate and anger with
Lessons, options, poems, affirmations
What you felt on the surface was buried deep within
Far, far away from others' eyes
You pulled me through the gutter and smiled
Re-taught me how I love to dance, and asked
'Is everything alright?'

Out of the frying pan...

Careful, child! Don't let your dress blow up so much
You're too pretty, don't smile so much
Don't talk to these idle boys 'round here
Go to the shop and come straight back!
Stop the noise!
Go, get ready for church.
Don't walk back by yourself, *Johnny* will walk you home.
Go put on some more clothes!
Maas Tom coming to cut the yard.

Beware the hands of little boys, and eyes of larger men
Their words? Worse!
Keep your wits sharp. Whether you're 5, or 8, or 10

But what do I do when the friends to watch are of the same
kind?
From the same cloth?
Playing with me in the same pen of knives I ran into
To get away from the boys?

Moonlight

Beware the hungry dog that comes in the night
Watching young mangoes in your yard
Touching, waiting for them to ripe
For when you take him in, he will feast at your table
And later, bite them all

Mango Time

Me nuh drink *cawfee* tea
But a lemonade, spiked?
Why, yes… I'll take it
Half is just enough
Quenches my thirst without sending me reeling
Why then, do I feel so… drowsy? What have you put in there?
You smile.
You say I smell like mangoes… ripe and ready to be picked
But how do I taste?
Meanwhile, I am seeing stars and smelling wars
Curling over and clutching walls
Screams stuck in my throat
And soon, I am welcomed by a blanket
Dark
Naked
Itchy
Why is everyone laughing?
Is there vomit in my hair?
Grass on my flesh?
Asphalt burns under my feet?
How did I get here?
Where have I been?
Where did you go?
I thought I saw a gun, In fact I'm sure it's true
But as for memories, I have none to show
What happened last night, that night, is gone
I can scratch at my innards a million ways
And still, I'll never know.

Miss Joyfull

They call you names… like worthless, stupid, lazy
I don't see that
They call you crazy, but again, alas…
Your warmth and charm
Beautiful smile, loving heart
Kind, bright, watery eyes
An extrovert, a socialite – still
No mention of that
A stylish flirt, just a bit
An excellent writer, an inhumanly speedy typist
No stories of your *joie de vivre*'
Or mirth, or talent, or witticisms
Ringing judgments are all I hear, but
As long as I have a pen, a tongue
Your story and worth will carry on because
We all need love
Somewhere to belong
A seat at the table
Hugs a *tups*' too long
A place to fit, to rest, to jest
Without question
To feel worthy, interesting, accepted, shameless
Where there's someone, at least one, who gets to know
The core of who you really are
Your fire and light, your love, your life
To see your heart and learn your truths.

Rock x release – part II

Darling, come!
Take a seat
Have some tea
Deep breaths, still seas
Sunsets...
At ease
Let it go
Float away on the whispering breeze
The weight of the world is heavy
You can't fix it, won't undo it all
Lay it down
Step back, start on the inside
Take time to unplug, reflect
Detach, not distract
Be alone with your thoughts
Put it down
Connect to source
Meditate on beautiful things
And when you're ready to move, love, start again.

Negus, Rise!

I know you
I know, you re-member in your DNA
Your years of renaming
Buck breaking
Undertaking
Watching your friends and family fall before you
Crying
Losing
Dying within... meeting targets without
Used for target practice and examples of what not to do... rebel
Ripped away from the fruits of your loins
Watching your sons accept their fate
Their worth as punching bags and cattle
Dick-slanging maniacs made you, your woman, your daughters
kneel
Then locked you up for fighting back

Where Is your mother, love?
Where is your mother's love?

She watches in the shadows far away
Breath bated, unable to rescue you
Generations of helplessness and hot iron fights steel your resolve
Branding your identity
Pushing you to wander, aimlessly, to find the ends of your pain
The justice, acceptance and recognition all humans deserve,

HARD GAL FI DEAD

but you can never claim
Finding only hardship entrenched in your skin

As the bell tolls and the curtains fall
You wonder, is the slate now clean?
For the mixed-breed mixture of contempt, shame, superiority
And your forefathers' sinless sin?

Trauma wreaks havoc on your brain and makes holes in your self-
esteem
You try to bleach out the stains of 400 years ago
Stains made of stab wounds, bullet holes, cat-o-nine tears and
disdain passed on through Genome manifested into flesh
And yet

Where is your salve?
Where is your chance?

Society fails you incessantly
And now the drum beats on but you don't even feel it
When do you loosen up?
When can you dance? Smile? Take the armour off your mind?
The same beat that nurtured your heart from the inside
The one you knew so well
The redness that comforted you
Was lost
They shoved your bonding down the throats of teething
oppressors who would later bite your heel
Choke you to death and call you coons, smiling

But wait, black man
You were born of the Eve gene
They cannot kill you, you mutate still
Do not let them absorb you,

HARD GAL FI DEAD

Keep fighting, realising, jumping ship to arrive home on the other
side of all of this

Break the chain, cut the rope, straighten your crown, for you are
king and we who nurtured you outside this dimension, will love
you back to life
Soothe you with flowers, honey, bush tea and gold
Magic
Melanated hugs and soul-stirring words
Feed you on wisdom; quench your thirst with health
Reverse old poisons with the kiss of life, comforting all souls within
you
Souls to come, souls still crying out from the sea

You are worth it!
A treasure, not a burden
A talent in an unfair game
But that is about to change
The time is now, Negus
Step into the sun… and rise.

Full Cup of Wombman

Beautiful
Strong
Powerful
Vulnerable
Wombman

Worthy
Driven
Anxious
Creative
Wombman

Stoic
Compassionate
Intelligent
Self-conscious
Hilarious
Basket-case
Wombman

Talented
Nurturing
Loving
Brave
No-longer-codependent
Wombman

Insecure
Empathic
Wombman
Confident
Wombman
Anti-social
Wombman
Shit-talking
Intuitive
Weird-humour-having
Never sleeping
Forever hungry
Wombman

Enigmatic
Wombman
Amazing
Wombman
Magnificent
Wombman
Wild
Wonderful
Crazy
Clairvoyant
Passive-aggressive
Wombman

Childlike
Hypercritical
Tantalising
Financially unstable
Wombman

Gorgeous
Alluring
Fearful
Sarcastic wombman
Neglected wombman
Self-nurturing wombman
Underestimated wombman
Misjudged wombman
Tactless, irreverent, easily distracted, wombman

Forgetful, impatient, big-belly woman
Sexy, magnetic, self-sacrificing wombman

Spiritual woman
Acidic wombman
Advocate and activist
Confused and uncharted wombman

Sad girl, vibrant wombman
Sage loving, incense burning, Palo Santo-having,
Oil sniffing, beach going, no swimming or driving wombman

Always writing wombman
Planning, dreaming, reviewing, believing wombman
Country girl, Maroon-rooted wombman
Native American Moorish wombman
European splashed wombman

Gifted, strange, absolutely weird wombman
Cruel wombman
Loved wombman
Christ-conscious wombman

HARD GAL FI DEAD

Took forever to embrace herself, now overflows with being
Wombman
Ever loving, ever faithful, ever evolving wombman...
I am that, I am.

A Limerick.

There's something compressing the air
Go ahead and poke fun if you dare
It was warm and then hot
It was silent, then not
Now it's causing the whole room to stare.

Notes to Self…

HARD GAL FI DEAD

I.   Dear Self,

You are magnificent. Created uniquely by God as a reflection of divinity. There is greatness in you by default, why must you doubt yourself so? When you were a baby, you were confident, you knew nothing else. You had no doubts; you questioned nothing on the inside. All your enquiries were about the fascinating world outside of you.

If you wanted something, you went after it. Without suspicion, you picked it up, played with it, put it into your mouth. When you loved something, you treasured it; you carried it everywhere, cried when you lost it...slept with it at night. You reached for it without hesitation simply because it looked interesting.

Why don't you do that anymore? There were no limits to your imagination and expectations, yet today, it is not so. Reconnect with your innocent, child-like confidence.

Do what you love, now. Start with what you have and do all you can to manifest your dreams today...it is the only time you have.

II.   Dear Self,

As clichéd as it may sound, if you never ask for what you want, the answer will always be no.

If you are not clear about your needs, your expectations, or your desires, then you are not being fair to yourself. Clarity fosters focus, which makes planning and dreaming easier. There is power in writing things down. It becomes an intention and the universe aligns with you to get it done. Remember this, my love, then look yourself in the eyes and say these words in the mirror every day...

The possibilities are endless for me because I believe in reciprocity. I am going to ask for what I want, because I deserve it, and I know that when the time is right, I will receive it.

III.   Dear Self,

I'm so proud to say that after years of struggle, I've learned to love you very much. I admire your strength, resilience and passion. I even love your empathy – although it seems to know no bounds. You've endured so much in your years of life. So much pain, loss, sadness, failures, abandonments, self-issues and self-inflicted wounds... yet, still you RISE. You are still here!

Living, loving, inspiring and, most of all, learning... evolving. 'Upping the ante'. You are constantly renewing and vibrating at a higher frequency and so, you know now, exactly who you are.

You know what you want. You know what inspires you, what turns you on (and off), and who you want to be.

You've learned the importance of leaving the past in the past. Whatever your mistakes, you're learning to forgive them because you understand now that you were different then.

Back then, you knew no better. Your life today has truly changed, so forget the wrongs and know that you did the best you could at that time with the resources, knowledge, faculties and experiences that you had then. Forgive yourself and let it go. It's time to move on now. God loves you and forgave you ages ago, so why remain stuck?

Put the bags down and walk away empty handed and free. Don't look back. Through trial and error, you taught yourself how to love. Now teach yourself how to truly live. Be in the moment and enjoy the cyclical nature of life. Go ahead, light being, it's okay. No need for guilt. Do whatever you need to do – the power is yours. Curse, swear, cry, stretch, sleep, run, sing, scream, breathe. Write it all down, and then, finally, decide to just let it go.

IV.   Dear Self,

Here's how you win...
    See it, feel it, love it, claim it, believe it, manifest it, accept it.
    What should be yours will always be yours.
    The truth always is.
    The people who are meant to stay, will.
    God has already ordained it.
    Abundance is for all of us, no need to think of lack,
    Or loss.
    You are the common denominator, remember that!
    It starts and ends with you – always.
    Fear is a distraction, designed to cripple, stagnate and
infuse doubt –
    By who else but you?
    Why? When the universe supports you readily...
    Everything you want is waiting out there for you to claim.
    Now, go ahead and do it.

V.   Dear Self

I have a challenge for you. It's a two-pronged task, and you must do it every day.

Remember those apologies you didn't get, and most likely, never will?

How about those people you thought you could never live without?

Or the disappointments that made you feel as though the world was ending?

Yes, those…

I want you to realise that you are here now, in this very moment because those things were never meant to work out for you, they weren't meant to be darling, that's why they didn't.

VI.   Dear Self,

You are enough.
You belong.
You are amazing and magnificent,
Smart, beautiful and kind.
Your life has meaning... purpose.
You are worthy of love.
You are worth being cherished and making an effort for.
<u>You are not a burden</u>.
You are a gift... a miracle, moonchild.
A wonderful and welcome cosmic surprise.
You couldn't be sexier or more awesome if you tried.
My dear, you are certainly not destined to fail, but know this; you and only you are responsible for your life.
You have it within you to create, so you can make your life great.
Create that! No one can tell you who you are and what your life is meant to be.
You are meant to be here, so BE HERE.

VII.   Dear Self,

You really need to be more mindful. Stop being so hard on YOU. Stop judging yourself so much. Watch your internal conversations and stop with the negative self talk. Instead, start to purposefully encourage yourself. Learn to understand yourself better, not explain yourself. Stop with the Goddamn 'pity party' and get out the fucking room.

As harsh as it sounds, it's time.

It's been time.

Focus on what you can control. Review how you're viewing things. Manage your expectations. Pick three things you hate most about your life right now and go about changing them. Make the steps, start figuring it out. Do something, anything but lie in bed.

You are already on your way. You cannot stay in here forever and you're doing the best you can with the resources you have right now, so just keep going and remember that you're human. Life will not be fantastic all the time, and that's okay. The 'lows' are part of the life cycle, just as the high points are. Life's not all about money, possessions or achievements.

You already have everything you need to survive and thrive, and things will work out as they should – like always.

VIII.   Dear Self,

Here are some simple things that cheer you up for those times when you forget:
- ✓ Awesome new music (and old faves)
- ✓ Cotton swabs
- ✓ Light rain
- ✓ Clouds
- ✓ Petrichor
- ✓ Sunrises...sunsets
- ✓ The moon
- ✓ Dark chocolate
- ✓ Earthing with Pachamama
- ✓ Bubble wrap
- ✓ Starry nights
- ✓ Writing
- ✓ Beach walks
- ✓ Animals
- ✓ Owls
- ✓ Cat videos

You're welcome.

IX.   Dear Self,

Love more.
Go after your dreams.
How?
Find out what they are, then outline them meticulously and pursue them relentlessly.
Hold yourself to achieving them as fiercely and passionately as you've done before for so many others.
Be enthusiastic about your life, it is your time to shine.

X.   Dear Self,

Just get over it. Seriously. Let it go. Life is so much easier when there's less things on your mind.

Do you remember ever feeling incredibly stressed out at age five? If something bad happened, wouldn't you just cry and get over it immediately? What's with this latching on to every little thing now? Time to simplify your life – go minimal. If someone or something bothers you that much, do what five-year-old you would do and immediately get away from it.

You have always known and will always know deep down the things and people that aren't right for you, just like you did when you were a child.

The only thing that's changed is time, and if anything, your intuition has only grown sharper.

The years are short, even when the days never seem to end. Life's too short to entertain discomfort, toxicity and unhappiness.

Make a conscious effort to hold on to good vibes and great moments. It really is that simple, even when it isn't.

XI.   Dear Self,

Forgiving others is great, but, what about you?

Don't be so quick to hold yourself to ransom. You can't pour from an empty cup, or light yourself on fire in the hope that the smoke kills the other person. . . so - to have good relationships with others - you must first have a great one with yourself, as clichéd as it sounds.

You're always quick to clear the air and seek closure with others. . . isn't it time you applied this principle to yourself?

Take the lesson and move on, enjoy life. Remember what Mama said, 'forgiveness doesn't mean you forget, it means when you remember, you no longer experience the same hurt feelings because you already let it go in your heart.   Profound, right? Try it.

ABOUT THE AUTHOR

Tameka A. Coley (Tami Tsansai) is a Jamaican writer and creative who uses her gifts to connect with and uplift others.
A self-proclaimed 'Blogtivist', she employs and promotes writing, reading, holistic living and creative expression as tools of self-discovery, self-care, social justice and freedom.

Tami has been weaving words into stories, poems and plays from as early as six years old. Writing was her first imaginative outlet, and after receiving a diary as a gift at age nine, it soon became her primary means of self-expression, exploration and therapy. Embracing the power of journalling and poetry early, it was a welcome relief from the turbulent, unexpressed emotions in her formative years. This remained handy right into adulthood as she periodically battled severe bouts of suicidal depression.

A fateful journey to studying Literatures in English led to unearthing her purpose —using her voice and artistic talents to make a meaningful contribution; speak up for under-served, stigmatised people, and raise awareness about the importance of mental health, self-actualisation and the relationship between both and achieving overall wellness. She continues to explore all facets of creative expression, work on empowering women of African descent, and building a mentally healthy, supportive community (both on and offline) through her *#MindBeingWellness* blog and social media (@tamitsansai).

TAMI TSANSAI

38272259R00076

Made in the USA
Columbia, SC
05 December 2018